# Violin Online String Sampler

*Violin Sheet Music*

By Robin Kay Deverich

Global Music School String Publications

Graphic Design by Julia Kay

ISBN 9780982170502

Copyright © 2008 Robin Kay Deverich. All Rights Reserved.

*No part of this publication may be reproduced in any form*
*or by any means without the prior written permission of the author.*

http://www.violinonlinestringsampler.com

# TABLE OF CONTENTS

## EARLY VIOLIN

| | COMPOSERS | |
|---|---|---|
| Columba aspexit | Hildegard of Bingen | 8 |
| *Sixth Royal Estampie* from Chansonnier du Roy | Anonymous | 9 |
| Helas Madame | King Henry 8th | 10 |
| Kemp's Jigg | Anonymous | 11 |
| Fantasia | Thomas Lupo | 12 |
| *Minuet* from The Fiddle New Model'd | Robert Crome | 13 |

## BAROQUE PERIOD

| | | |
|---|---|---|
| *Rondeau* from Abdelazar | Henry Purcell | 18 |
| *Hornpipe* from Water Music Suite | George Frideric Handel | 19 |
| La Folia medley | Marin Marais, Arcangelo Corelli, Antonio Vivaldi | 20 |
| Double Violin Concerto in A Minor, Op. 3, No. 8, 1st movement | Antonio Vivaldi | 22 |
| *Prelude* from Cello Suite I in G Major | J.S. Bach | 24 |
| *Allegro* from Brandenburg Concerto No. 5 | J.S. Bach | 26 |
| *Kyrie* from Messa a 4 con violini | Maurizio Cazzati | 28 |
| Medley: *He Shall Feed His Flock Like a Shepherd* and *Hallelujah Chorus* from Messiah | George Frideric Handel | 30 |
| *Arioso* from Cantata No. 156 | J.S. Bach | 32 |

## CLASSICAL PERIOD

| | | |
|---|---|---|
| Ave Verum Corpus, K. 618 | Wolfgang Amadeus Mozart | 33 |
| *Adagio* from Violin Concerto No. 3 in G | Wolfgang Amadeus Mozart | 34 |
| *Andante* from String Quartet No. 13 in Am | Franz Schubert | 36 |
| *Andante* from Emperor Quartet in C major | Franz Joseph Haydn | 37 |
| Surprise Symphony No. 94, 2nd movement | Franz Joseph Haydn | 38 |
| Pastoral Symphony No. 6, 1st and 5th movements | Ludwig van Beethoven | 39 |

## ROMANTIC PERIOD

| | | |
|---|---|---|
| Hungarian Dance No. 5 | Johannes Brahms | 40 |
| *The Moldau* from Ma Vlast. | Bedrich Smetana | 41 |
| *Halling* from 25 Norwegian Folksongs and Dances | Edward Grieg | 42 |
| Emperor Waltz | Johann Strauss II | 43 |
| Vieille Chanson | Pauline Viardot | 44 |
| *Andante* from Violin Concerto in E Minor | Felix Mendelssohn | 46 |
| *Allegro* and *Adagio* from B minor Cello Concerto | Antonin Dvorak | 47 |
| *Nocturne* from String Quartet No. 2 in D major | Alexander Borodin | 48 |
| *Elégie* Op. 44 for Viola and Piano | Alexander Glazunov | 49 |
| *Barcarolla* from Sonata in Bb for Viola and Piano | Henri Vieuxtemps | 50 |
| *Ave Maria* from a theme by J.S. Bach | Charles Gounod/J.S. Bach | 51 |
| Sicilienne Op. 78 for cello and piano | Gabriel Fauré | 52 |
| *Meditation* from Thaïs | Jules Massenet | 54 |
| *Habanera* from Carmen | Georges Bizet | 56 |
| *Reed Flutes* from The Nutcracker Suite | Pyotr Ilyich Tchaikovsky | 57 |

## 20th CENTURY

| | | |
|---|---|---|
| *Overture* from Pulcinella Ballet | Igor Stravinsky | 58 |
| *Moderato* from Sonata No. 1 in G Major | Domenico Gallo | 60 |
| *Assez vif* from String Quartet in F Major | Maurice Ravel | 62 |
| *Sehr langsam* from 4 Pieces, Op. 7 | Anton Webern | 63 |
| Simple Gifts melody | Joseph Brackett Jr. | 64 |
| *Braul* from Romanian Folk Dances | Bela Bartok | 65 |

## NON-TRADITIONAL

| | | |
|---|---|---|
| The Basso | Gypsy Traditional | 66 |
| Odessa Bulgarish | Klezmer Traditional | 67 |
| Varys Hasapikos | Greek Traditional | 68 |
| El Jarabe Tapatio | Mexican Traditional | 69 |
| Jasmine Flower | Chinese Traditional | 70 |
| Sara Sara | Tyāgarāja (Carnatic) | 71 |
| Longa Nahawand | Tanburi Cemil Bey (Arabic/Ottoman) | 72 |
| *Fiddle Medley:* Bile Them Cabbage Down, Devil's Dream and Shuffle | Fiddle Traditional | 73 |
| Irish Washerwoman | Irish Traditional | 75 |
| The Ragtime Violin | Irving Berlin | 76 |
| The Castle Walk | James Reese Europe & Ford T. Dabney | 77 |
| St. Louis Blues | W. C. Handy | 79 |

# Preface

*Violin Online String Sampler Violin Sheet Music* features 54 violin pieces representing styles from a variety of music history periods and cultures, including Medieval, Renaissance, Baroque, Classical, Romantic, 20$^{th}$ Century, Fiddle, Klezmer, Gypsy, Chinese, Greek, Carnatic, Arabic, Mariachi, Ragtime and Blues. These arrangements have been simplified for advanced beginners to intermediate players (all of the music is in 1$^{st}$ position), and provide a representative sampling of most major forms of string music such as concertos, symphonies, sonatas, quartets and trios. A study guide, sold separately, explains the history and musical form of the selected pieces, and includes violin technique tips for each piece of music.

As an added bonus, sound files of each piece are currently available on a website* specifically designed to accompany this course: *http://www.violinonlinestringsampler.com*. Content from ViolinOnline™ is also provided on this site, including a review of violin basics such as instrument care and tuning; violin playing position; fingering assistance; violin technique tips; scales and etudes; and music theory basics.

Making music can bring you joy, and this string sampler is designed to help you actively learn, study and play beautiful string music from a wide variety of styles and eras. Let the music begin!

*No guarantees are made that these sound files and website will be available indefinitely.*

# Columba aspexit

Hildegard

# Sixth Royal Estampie

Anonymous

# Helas madame

Henry VIII

# Kemp's Jigg

Anonymous

# Fantasia

Lupo

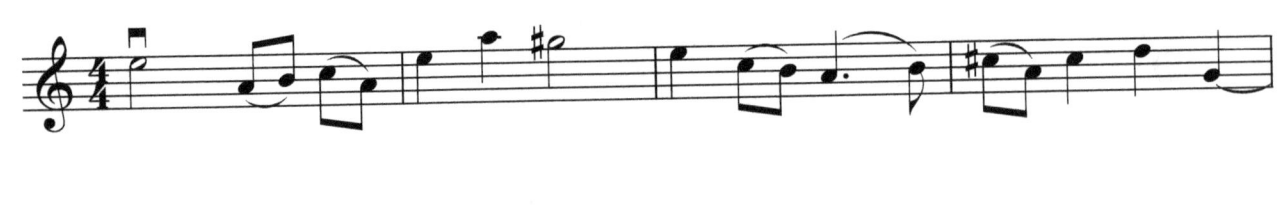

# Minuet & Finger Pattern 1

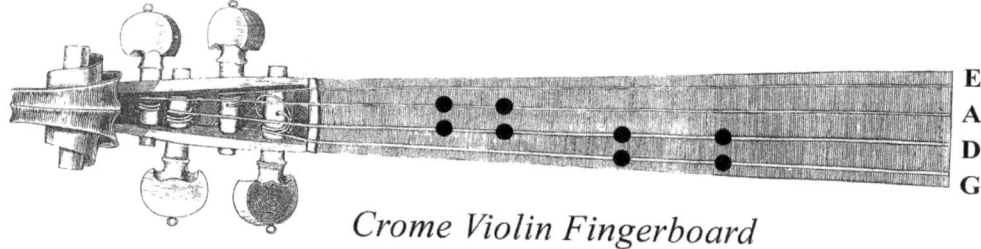

*Crome Violin Fingerboard*

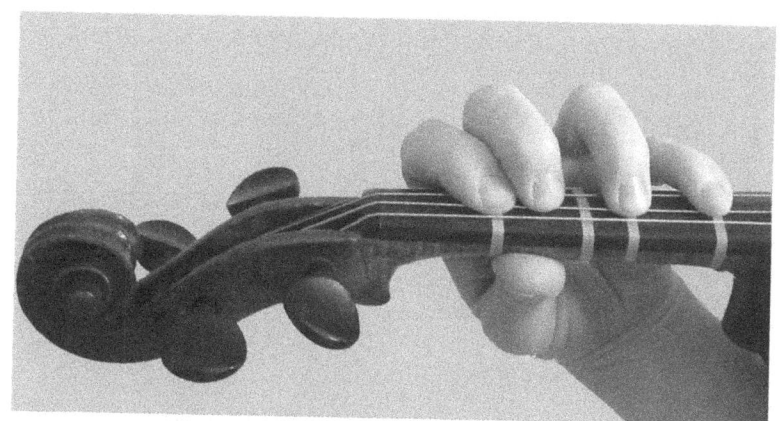

*Finger Pattern 1*

C Major Scale

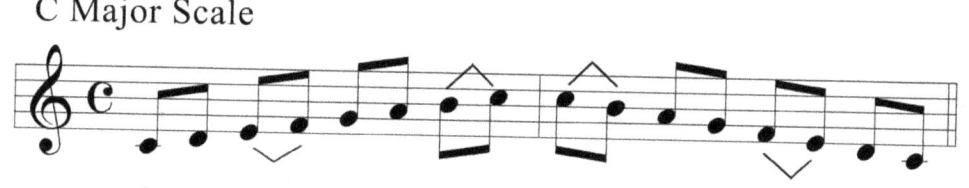

*The symbol ∧ or ∨ indicates that these fingers should be placed closely together*

## Minuet 1

Crome

# Minuet & Finger Pattern 2

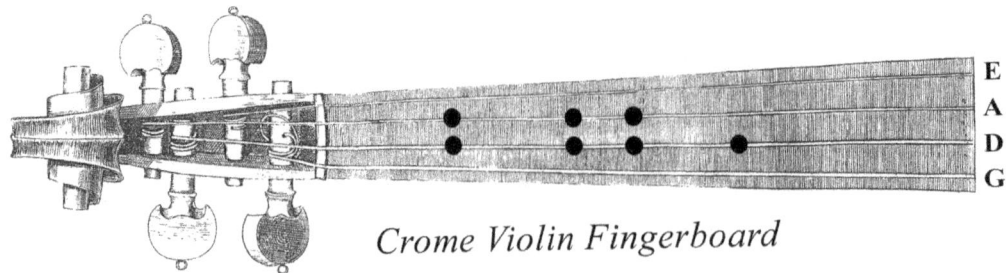

*Crome Violin Fingerboard*

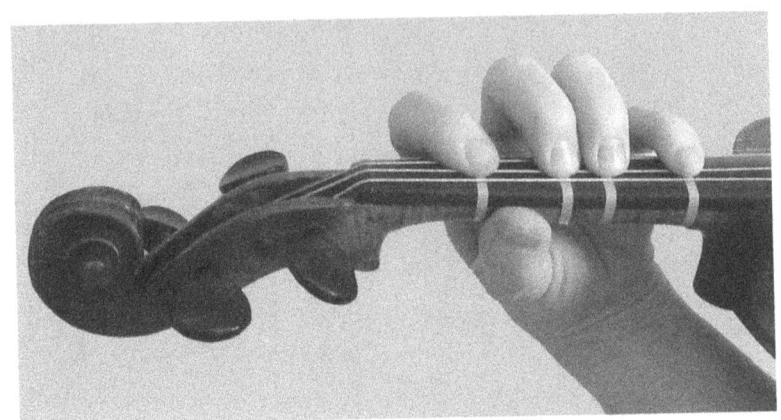

*Finger Pattern 2*

### D Major Scale

The symbol ∧ or ∨ indicates that these fingers should be placed closely together

## Minuet 2

Crome

# Minuet & Finger Pattern 3

*Crome Violin Fingerboard*

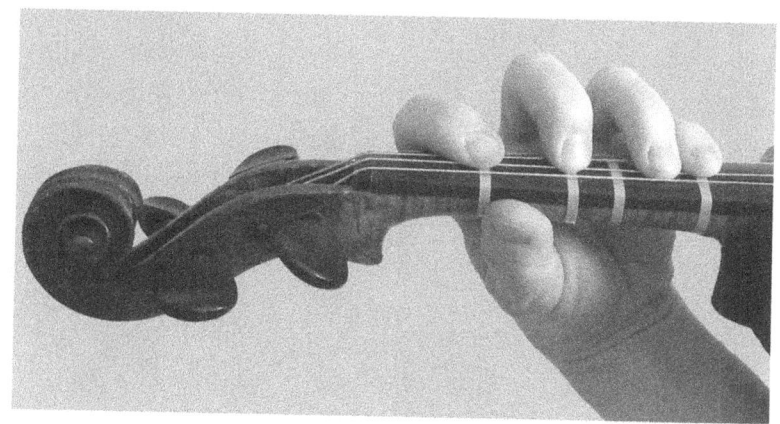
*Finger Pattern 3*

A Major Scale

The symbol ∧ or ∨ indicates that these fingers should be placed closely together

## Minuet 3
Crome

# Minuet & Finger Pattern 4

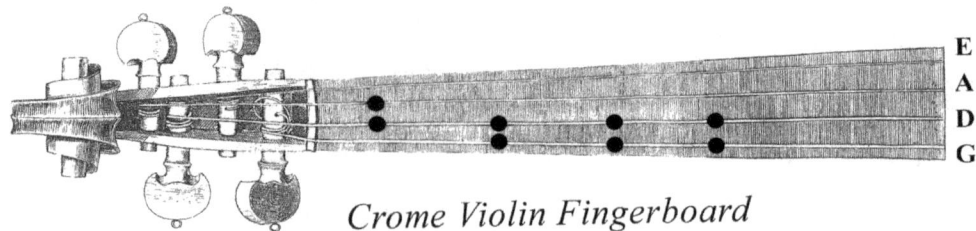

*Crome Violin Fingerboard*

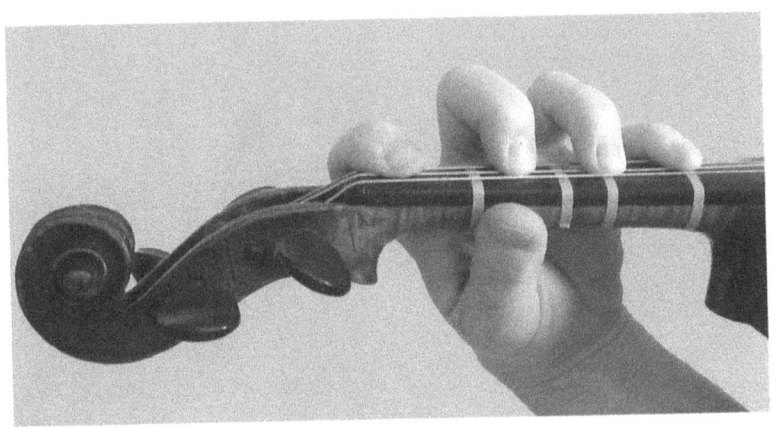

*Finger Pattern 4*

## Minuet 4

Crome

# Minuet & Finger Pattern 5

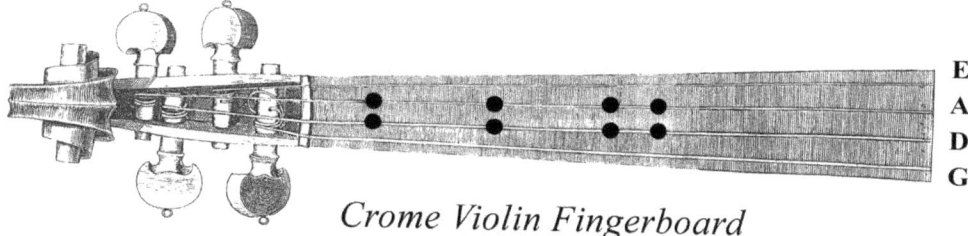

*Crome Violin Fingerboard*

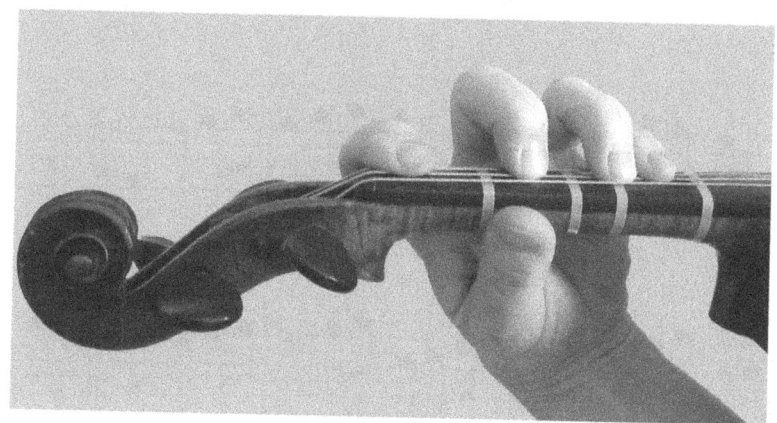

*Finger Pattern 5*

Eb Major Scale

The symbol ∧ or ∨ indicates that these fingers should be placed closely together

## Minuet 5

Crome

©2008 RK Deverich

# Rondeau

Purcell

# Hornpipe
*from Water Music Suite in D*

Handel

# La Folia

# Violin Concerto in A minor
## *1st Movement*

Vivaldi

# Prelude
*from Cello Suite No. 1*

Bach

# Allegro
*from Brandenburg Concerto No. 5*

Bach

# Kyrie

Cazzati

# Arioso

Bach

# Ave Verum Corpus

Mozart

# Adagio
*from Violin Concerto No. 3*

Mozart

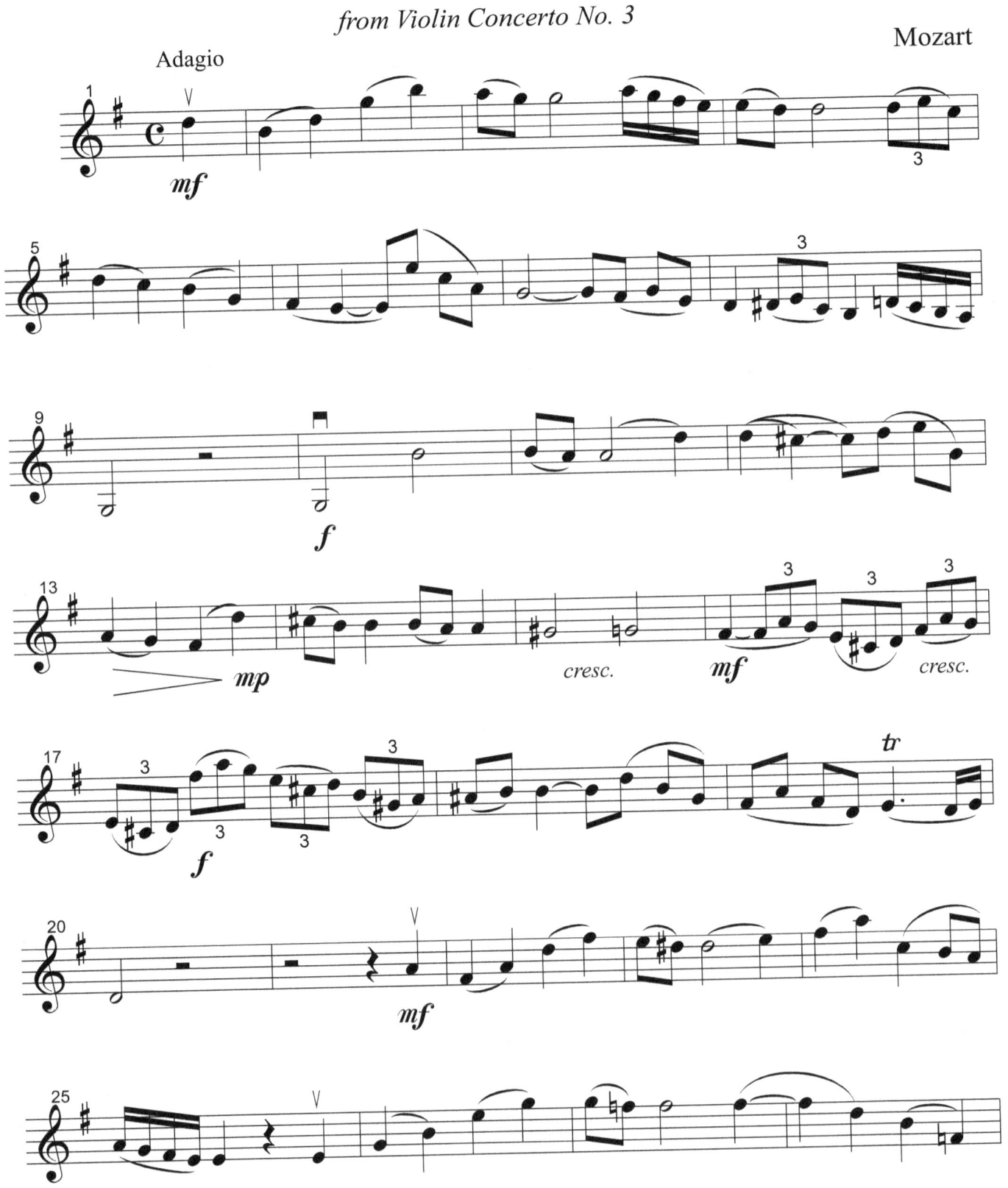

# Andante
*from String Quartet No. 13 in A minor*

Schubert

# Andante
*from the Emperor Quartet*

Haydn

Poco Adagio Cantabile

# Surprise Symphony

Haydn

# Pastoral Symphony No. 6

Beethoven

*Allegro* — The awakening of joyful feelings upon arriving in the country

# Hungarian Dance No. 5

Brahms

# The Moldau
*from Má vlast*

Smetana

# Halling

Grieg

# Emperor Waltz

Tempo di Valse

Strauss

# Vieille Chanson

Viardot

# Andante
*from Violin Concerto Op. 64*

Mendelssohn

# Cello Concerto in B Minor

Dvořák

# Nocturne
*from String Quartet No. 2*

Borodin

Andante *cantabile ed espressivo*

# Elégie

Glazunov

# Barcarolla

Vieuxtemps

*Andante*

*con melancolia*

# Ave Maria

Andante semplice

Bach-Gounod

# Sicilienne

Fauré

# Meditation
*from Thaïs*

Massenet

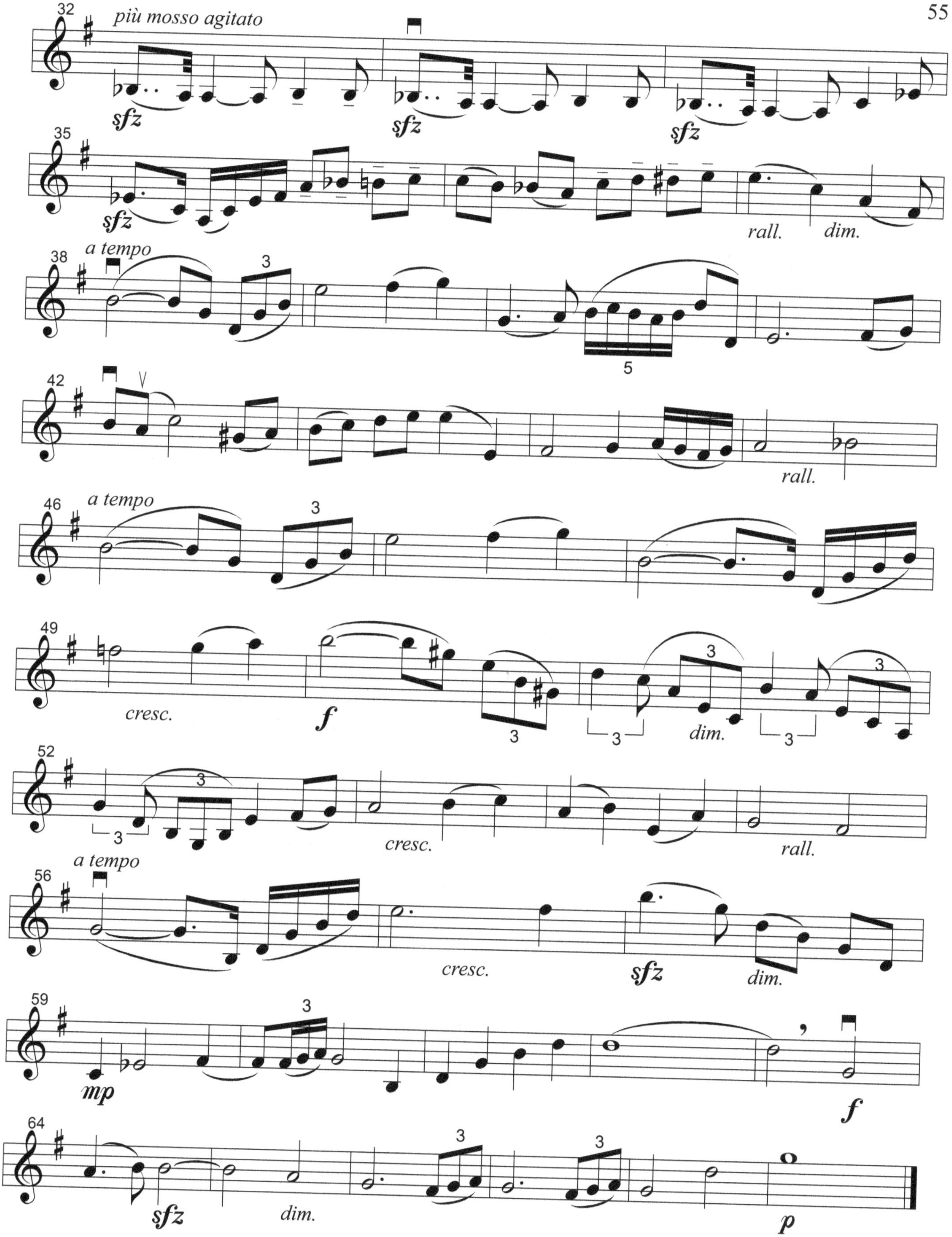
32
più mosso agitato
sfz
sfz
sfz
35
sfz
rall.
dim.
38
a tempo
42
rall.
46
a tempo
49
cresc.
f
dim.
52
cresc.
rall.
56
a tempo
cresc.
sfz
dim.
59
mp
f
64
sfz
dim.
p

# Habanera

Bizet

# Overture
*from Pulcinella*

Stravinsky

# Trio Sonata No. 1
*(originally attributed to Pergolesi)*

Moderato

Gallo

# Assez vif

*from Quartet in F*

Ravel

# Sehr langsam

*from 4 Pieces, Op. 7*

Webern

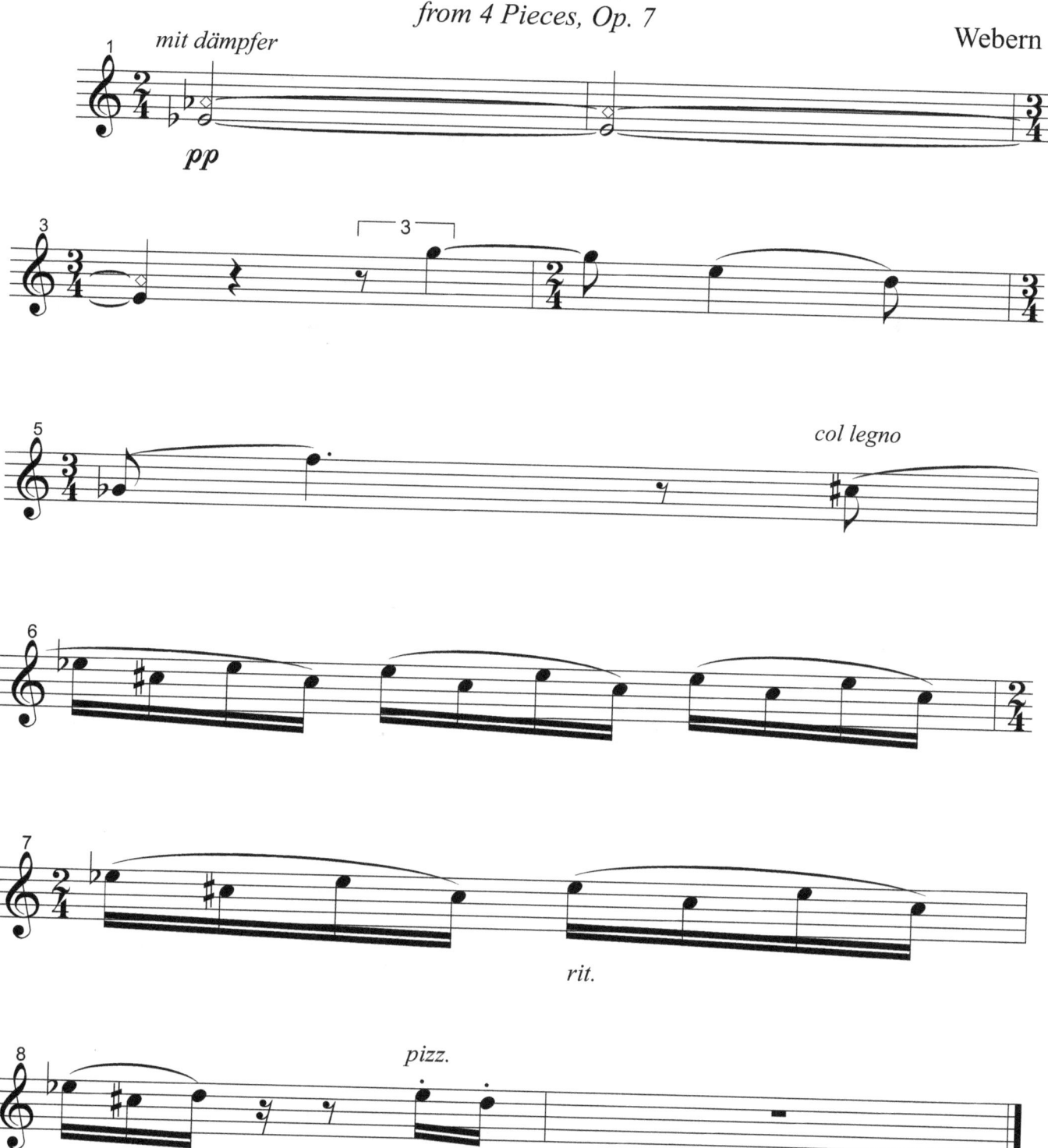

# Simple Gifts

Brackett

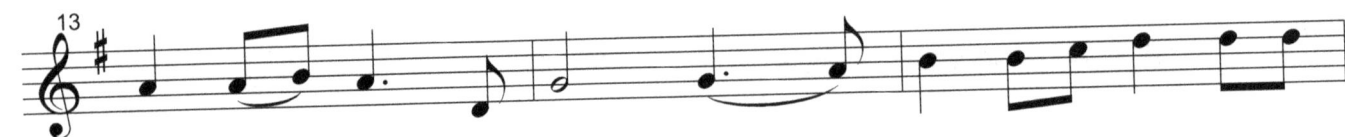

# Braul

Bartok

# The Basso

Gypsy Traditional

©2008 RK Deverich

# Odessa Bulgarish

*Klezmer Traditional*

# Varys Hasapikos

Greek Traditional

# El jarabe tapatío

Mexican Traditional

# Jasmine Flower

Chinese Traditional

*rit.*

# Fiddle Medley

©2008 RK Deverich

# Irish Washerwoman

Irish Traditional

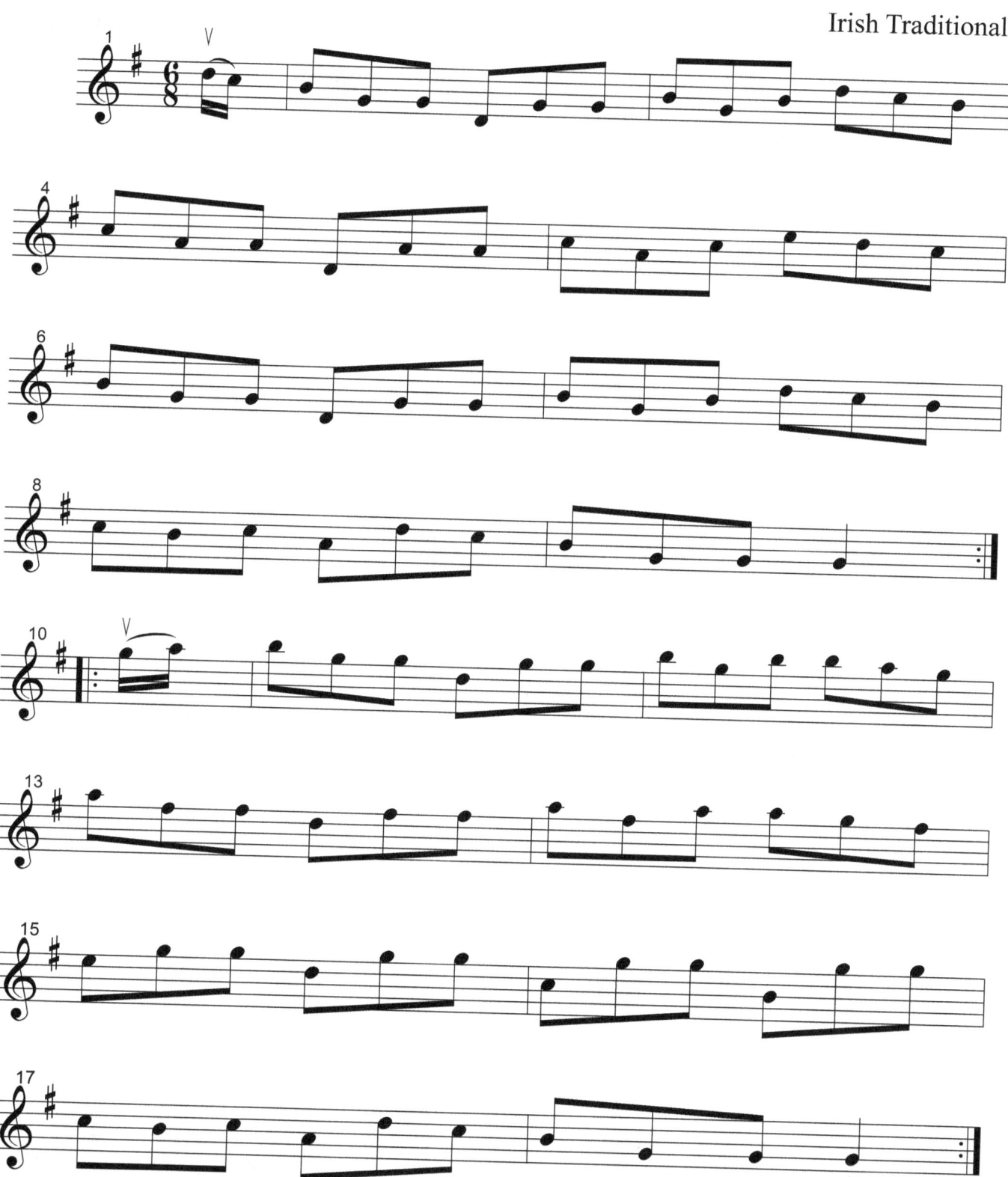

©2008 RK Deverich

# Ragtime Violin

Berlin

# The Castle Walk

Europe & Dabney

# St. Louis Blues

Handy

©2008 RK Deverich